Oboe

Progressive Musical Studies:

Sousa Grade 2-3

Compiled by Brian R. Thompson M.M.

ISBN 978-0-359-86042-5

About the Composer

Brian Thompson has been teaching band in rural Utah for the past 13 years. He was selected as a 2018 quarter finalist for **"Educator of the Year" by the Grammy Foundation.**

He has taught at Richfield High School and Red Hills Middle School until recently when he took the responsibility of teaching choir and band at the high school. Brian and his wife have four children.

Brian received a Associates Degree from Snow College, a Bachelor's of Music in Music Education from the University of Utah, and a Master's Degree in Instrumental conducting from Sam Houston State University through the American Band College in Ashland Oregon.

Brian has numerous arrangements for various small ensembles. He most enjoys arranging music for brass quintets, trombone quartets, percussion ensembles, and many others depending on what his students want to play and their abilities. You can find some of those at www.sevierband.com.

Foreward

The premise of this book is to teach musicality rather than just a single piece of music. Bands often spend too much time preparing one piece for performance, which is teaching to the test, and not enough time learning how to play music or, in other words, musicality.

Sight-reading does not teach students to play different styles. In sight-reading books, the exercises are not musical but teach notes and rhythms. Musicality includes the ability to play a melody, counter melody, accompaniment and a bass line all together, which can only be learned by playing real music. To learn musicality, students need to play many different pieces as they study not just the few for the concert.

John Philip Sousa's music is rich with musical examples. I spent a year studying hundreds of scores and found his music to be one of the best resources for showing musicality. The problem with Sousa's music: it is too hard and too long for most students. French horns learn to play rhythms and accompaniment well, but that is all they do. Tubas get great bass lines, but no one else does. The trumpet gets the melody but hardly anything else.

This book breaks down musical selections from Sousa's music to teach musicality. It is rated from easy to hard. Everyone in the band will have the opportunity to study all parts of the music, so they can begin to understand the melody, counter melody, accompaniment and a bass line. They can even divide into groups of five or six to play each of these selections together.

I wrote this book to teach music not just a single piece; to teach musicality not just articulation; to teach students to play expressively not just with dynamics; to teach students to listen vertically to the chords in accompaniment while playing a melody horizontally for phrasing.

Brian R. Thompson
Sevier Band & Percussion

Table of Contents

Progressive Musical Studies:

John Philip Sousa Grade 2-3.

Compiled by Brian R. Thompson M.M.

1

The Corcoran Cadets

Concert Oboe

2

Homeward Bound

Concert Oboe

3

The Thunderer

Concert Oboe

Second Strain 1889

John Philip Sousa
Arr. Brian R. Thompson

Melody

Counter Melody

Accompaniment

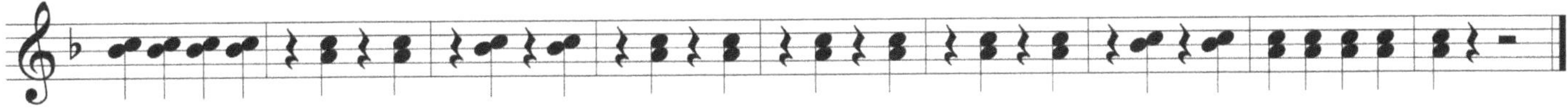

Bass

4

The Belle of Chicago

Concert Oboe

National Fencibles

Concert Oboe

Trio

1888

John Philip Sousa
Arr. Brian R. Thompson

Bass

Globe and Eagle (1879) — Intro

Sound Off

Concert Oboe

Break Strain

1885

John Philip Sousa
Arr. Brian R. Thompson

Melody

Bass

The Belle of Chicago (1892) — Intro

The Loyal Legion (1890) — Intro

7

Pet of the Petticoats

Concert Oboe

National Fencibles

Concert Oboe

Melody

Second Strain 1888

John Philip Sousa
Arr. Brian R. Thompson

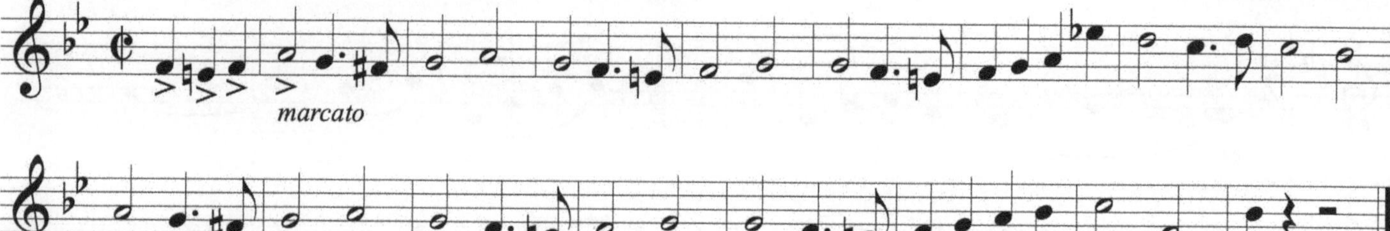

Accompaniment

Bass

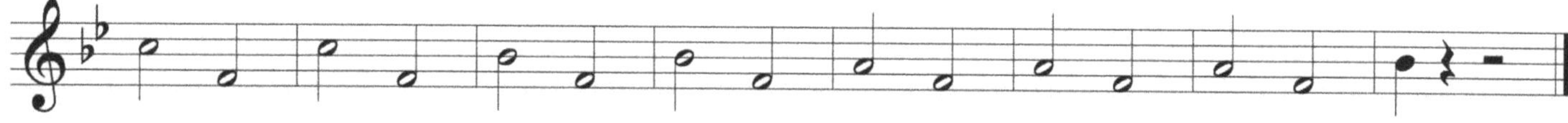

The Quilting Party (1889) — Intro

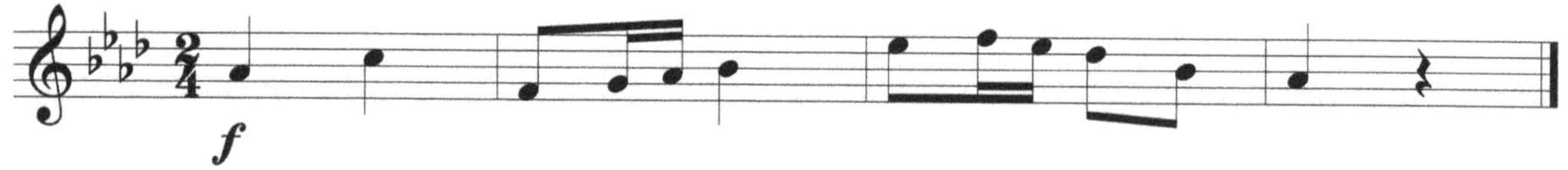

9

The White Plume

Concert Oboe

Second Strain 1884

John Philip Sousa
Arr. Brian R. Thompson

10

Bonnie Annie Laurie

Concert Oboe

Second Strain

1885

John Philip Sousa
Arr. Brian R. Thompson

11

Mother Goose

Concert Oboe

Trio Part 2 **1883**

John Philip Sousa
Arr. Brian R. Thompson

Melody

Harmony

Accompaniment

Bass

Mother Goose (1883) — Intro

Sound Off

Concert Oboe

Trio 1885

John Philip Sousa
Arr. Brian R. Thompson

Melody

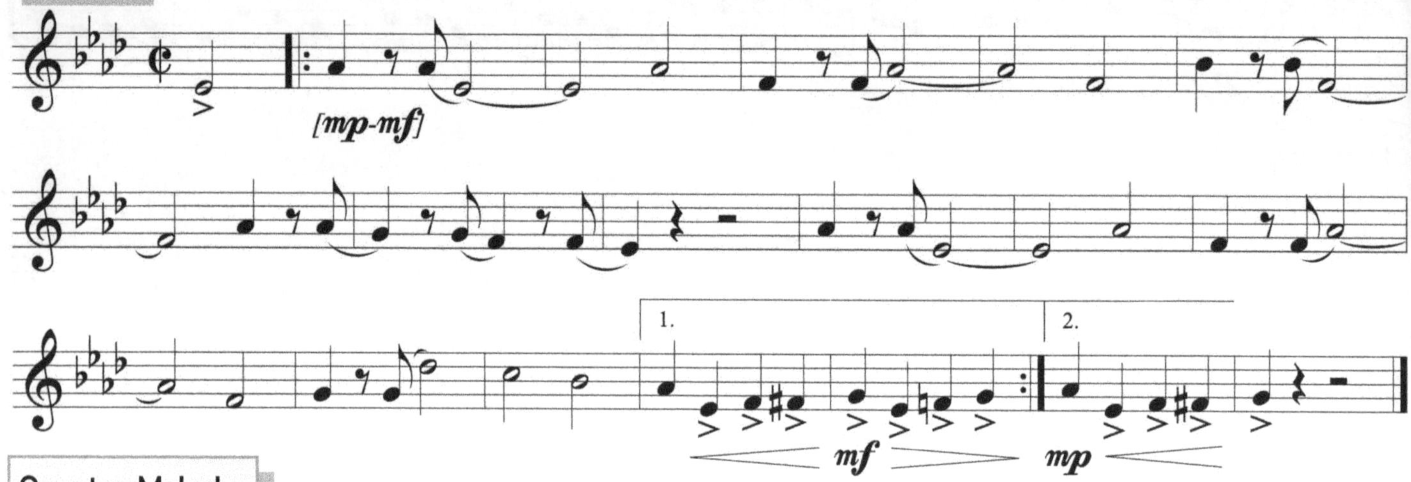

[mp-mf]

1. 2.

mf mp

Counter Melody

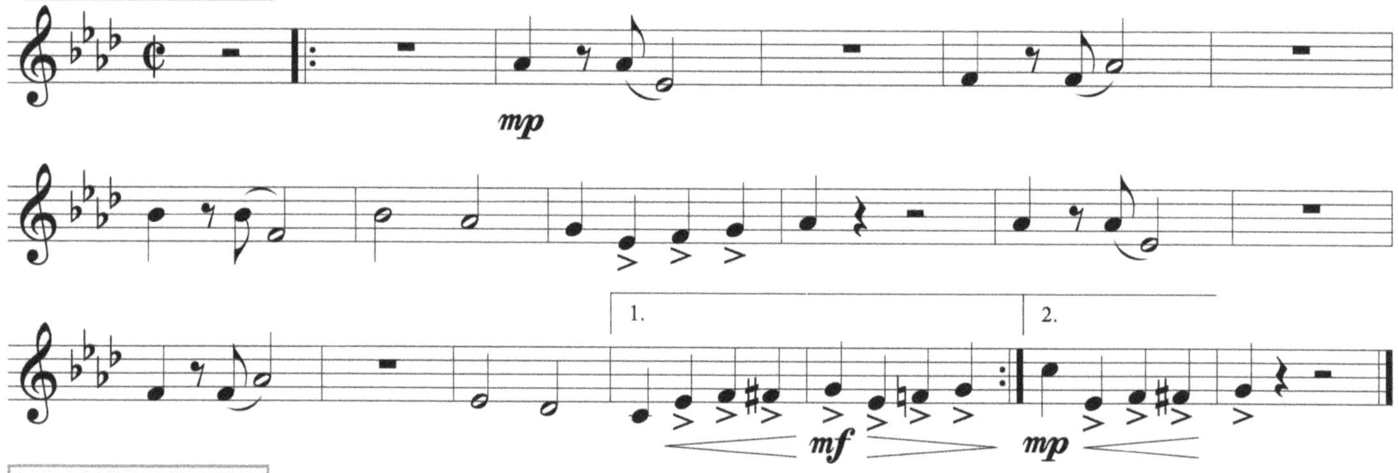

mp

1. 2.

mf mp

Accompaniment

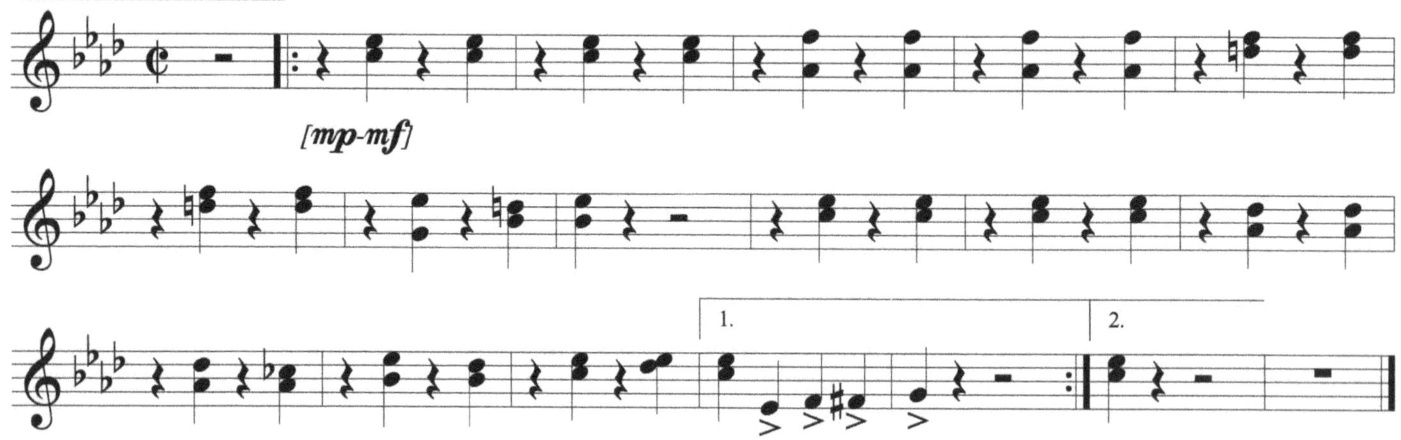

[mp-mf]

1. 2.

12b

Sound Off

Concert Oboe

Trio 1885

John Philip Sousa
Arr. Brian R. Thompson

Bass

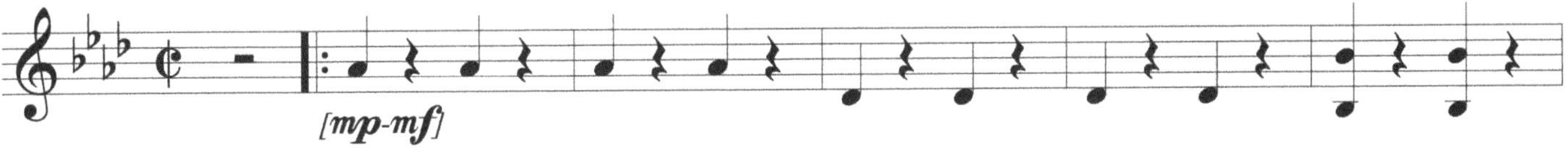

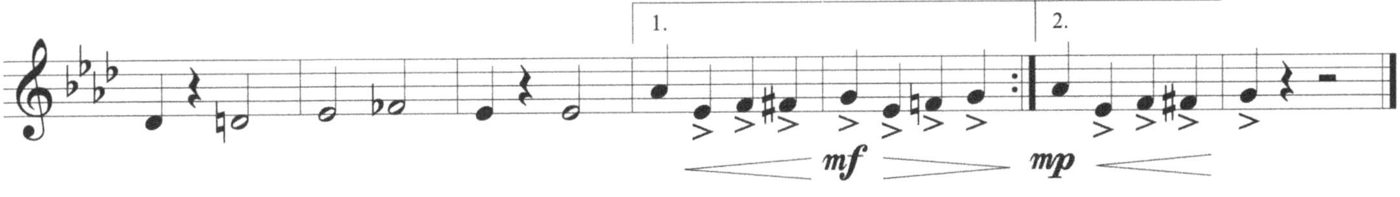

Corcoran Cadets (1890) — Break Strain

Mikado March (1885) — Intro

13

Mother Goose

Concert Oboe

Mother Hubbard

Concert Oboe

First Strain 1885

John Philip Sousa
Arr. Brian R. Thompson

15

Sound Off

Concert Oboe

Second Strain 1885

John Philip Sousa
Arr. Brian R. Thompson

Melody

Accompaniment

Accompaniment

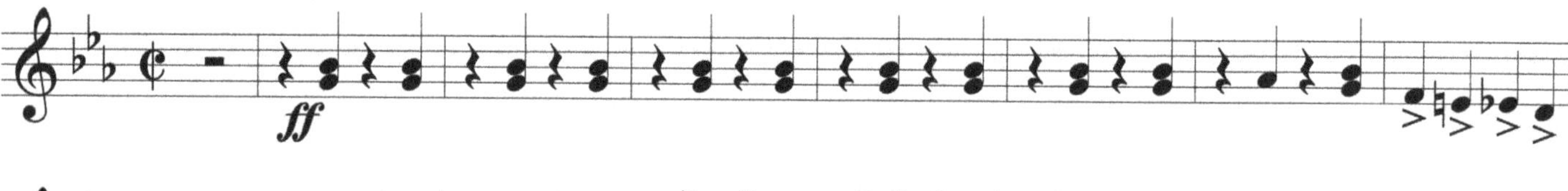

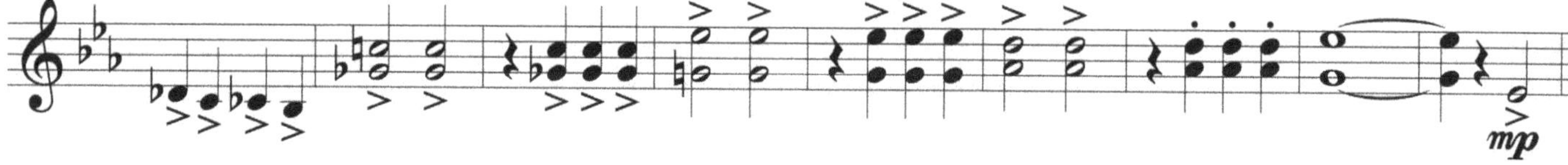

Bass

Mother Goose

Concert Oboe

First Strain 1883

John Philip Sousa
Arr. Brian R. Thompson

Melody

Accompaniment

Accompaniment

Bass

17

Homeward Bound

Concert Oboe

First Strain

1891-2

John Philip Sousa
Arr. Brian R. Thompson

Melody

mf

1. 2.

ff

Counter Melody

mf

1. 2.

ff

Accompaniment

mf

1. 2.

ff

Bass

mf

1. 2.

ff

The Triton

Concert Oboe

Trio 1892

John Philip Sousa
Arr. Brian R. Thompson

Melody

Counter Melody

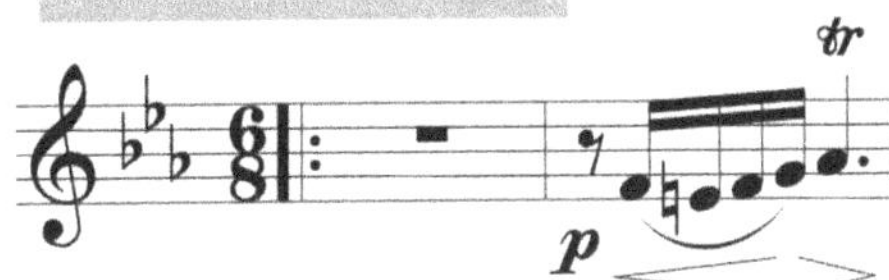

Accompaniment

Bass

The Thunderer (1889) — Intro

Part 1

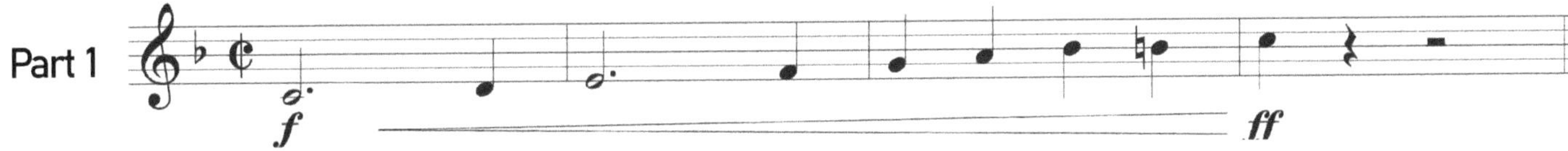

Part 2

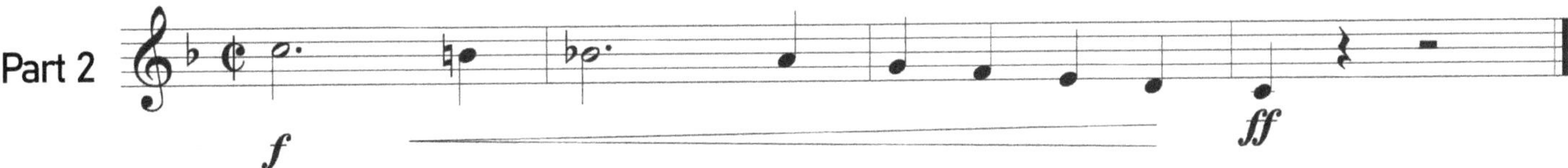

19

The Thunderer

Concert Oboe

First Strain

1889

John Philip Sousa
Arr. Brian R. Thompson

Melody

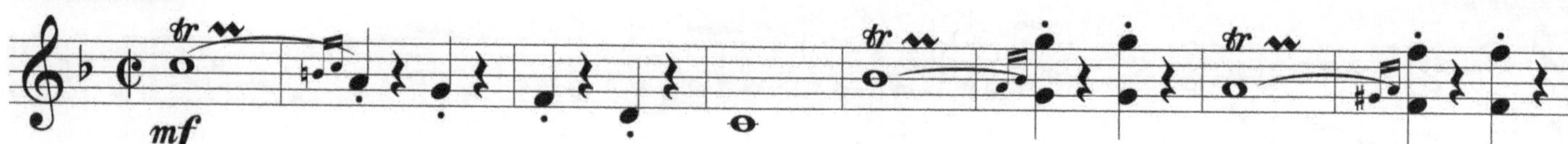

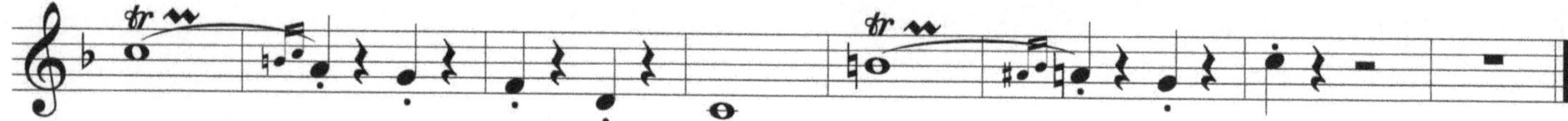

Counter Melody

Accompaniment

Bass

20

Mother Goose

Concert Oboe

Trio Part 1

1883

John Philip Sousa
Arr. Brian R. Thompson

Melody

Harmony

Accompaniment

20b

Mother Goose

Concert Oboe

Trio Part 1 1883

John Philip Sousa
Arr. Brian R. Thompson

Bass

Challenge

The Beau Ideal (1893) — Intro

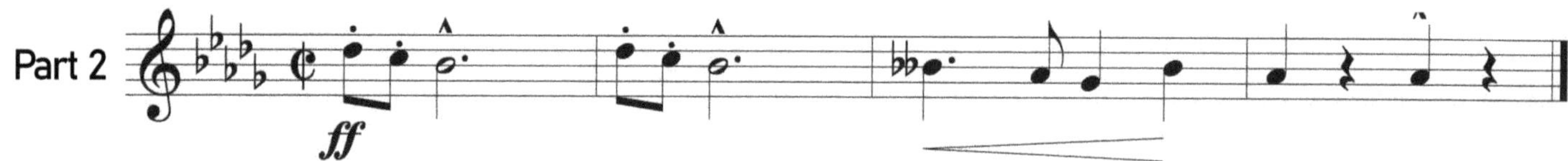

The Thunderer

Concert Oboe

Final Strain 1889

John Philip Sousa
Arr. Brian R. Thompson

22

The Belle of Chicago

Concert Oboe

22b

The Belle of Chicago

Concert Oboe

Trio 1892

John Philip Sousa
Arr. Brian R. Thompson

Bass

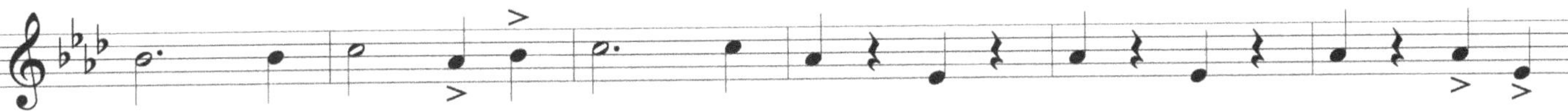

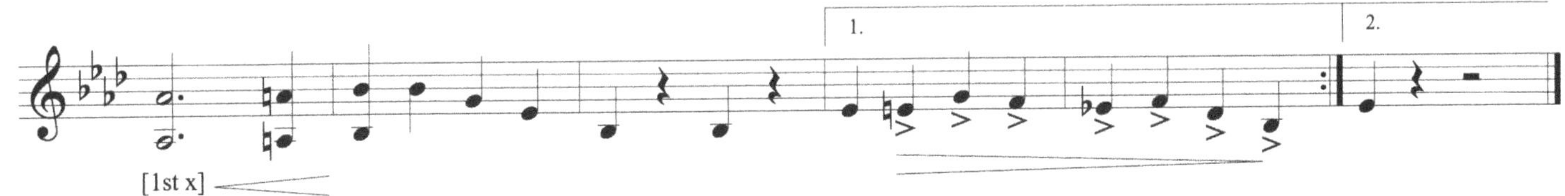

The Loyal Legion (1890) — Break Strain

Part 1

Part 2

23

Mother Goose

Concert Oboe

Melody

Trio Part 3

1883

John Philip Sousa
Arr. Brian R. Thompson

f

ff

Counter Melody

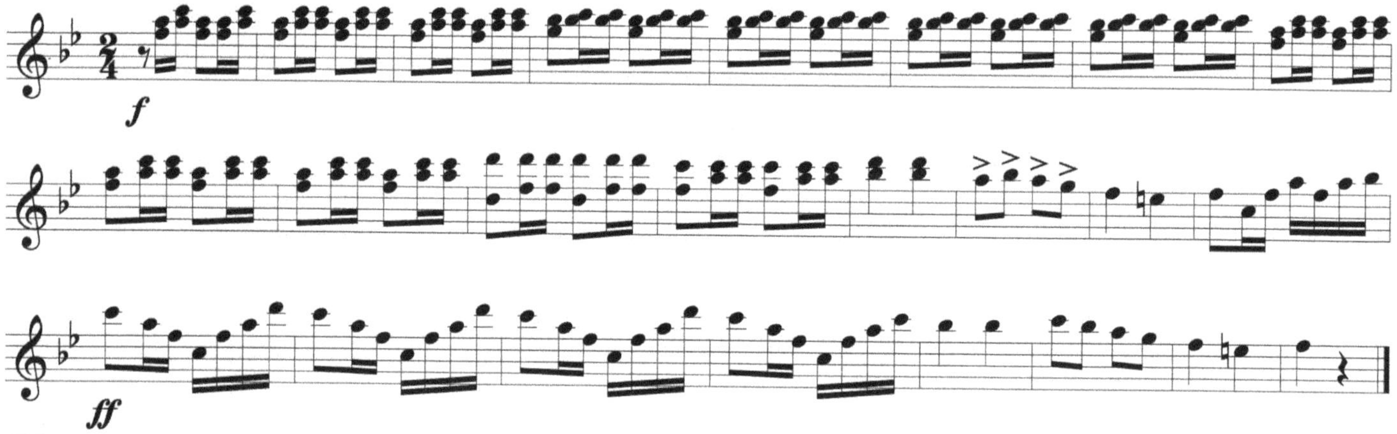

f

ff

Accompaniment

f

ff

23b

Mother Goose

Concert Oboe

Bass

Trio Part 3

1883

John Philip Sousa
Arr. Brian R. Thompson

Boy Scouts of America (1916) — Break Strain

Mikado March

Concert Oboe

Second Strain

1885

John Philip Sousa
Arr. Brian R. Thompson

Melody

Accompaniment

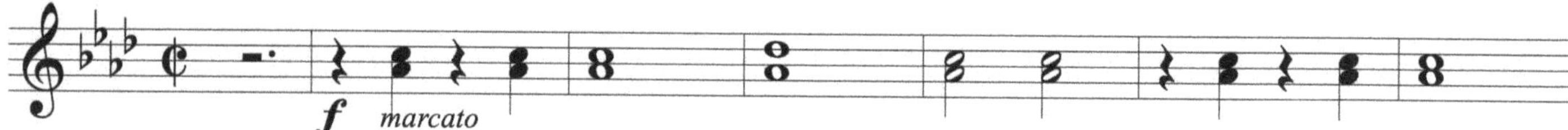

Accompaniment

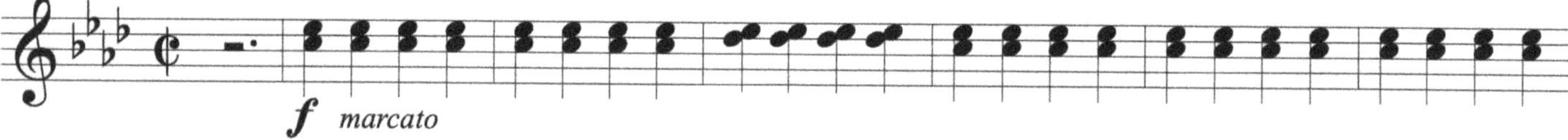

Bass

The Quilting Party

Concert Oboe

First Strain **1885**

John Philip Sousa
Arr. Brian R. Thompson

Melody

Accompaniment

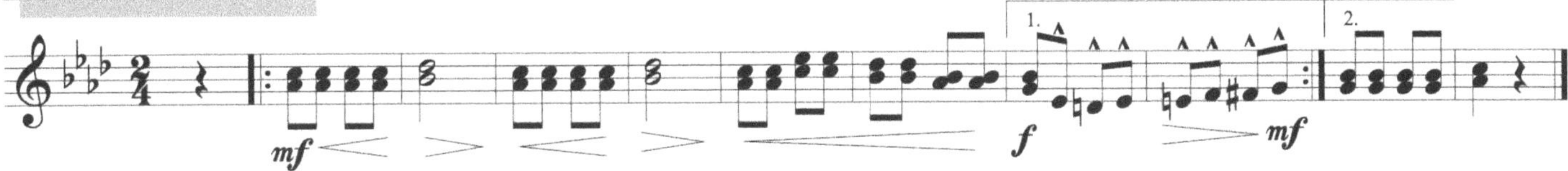

Accompaniment

Bass

Manhattan Beach (1893) — Intro

Part 1

Part 2

The High School Cadets

Concert Oboe

Mikado March

Concert Oboe

Final Strain 1885

John Philip Sousa
Arr. Brian R. Thompson

Melody

Accompaniment

Accompaniment

Bass

El Capitan

Concert Oboe

Trio 1896

John Philip Sousa
Arr. Brian R. Thompson

Melody

Harmony

Accompaniment

Accompaniment

28b

El Capitan

Concert Oboe

Trio 1896

John Philip Sousa
Arr. Brian R. Thompson

Bass

Yorktown Centennial (1881) — Bugle Strain

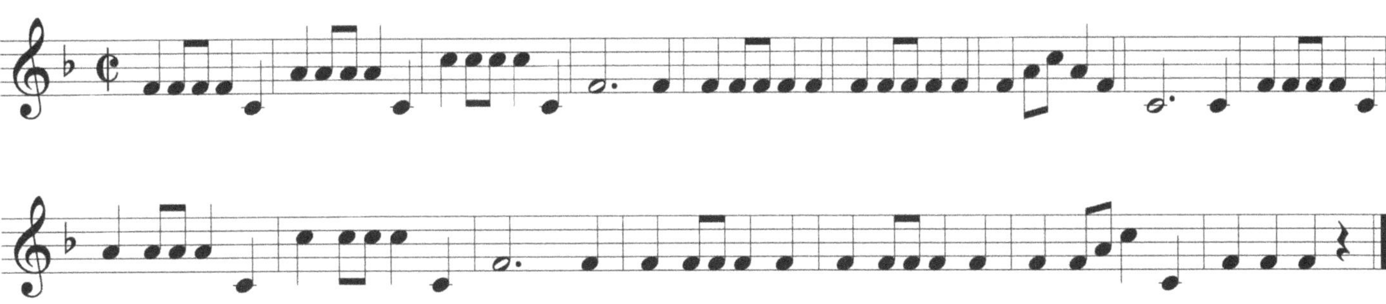

Bonnie Annie Laurie (1883) — Intro

29

The Washington Post

Concert Oboe

29b

The Washington Post

Concert Oboe

Second Strain 1889

John Philip Sousa
Arr. Brian R. Thompson

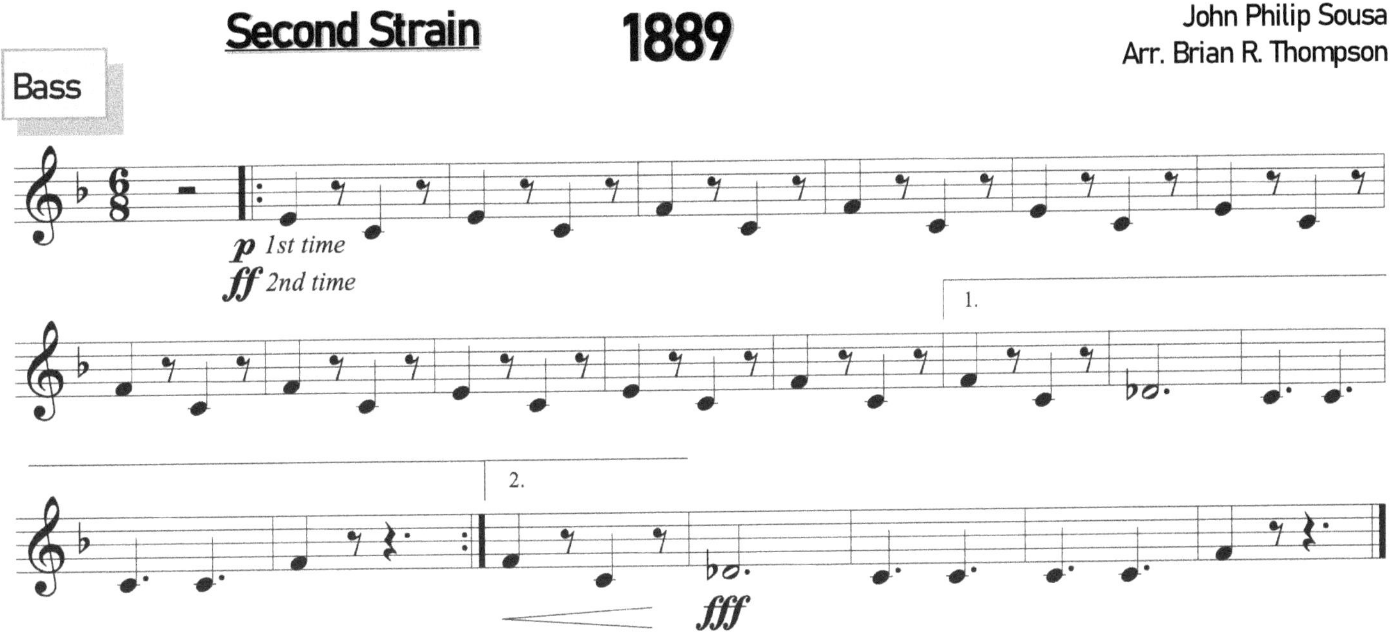

Pet of the Petticoats (1883) — Break Strain

Revival (1876) — Intro

30

Sabre and Spurs

Concert Oboe

Trio 1918

John Philip Sousa
Arr. Brian R. Thompson

Melody

Accompaniment

Accompaniment

31

The Diplomat

Concert Oboe

First Strain 1904

John Philip Sousa
Arr. Brian R. Thompson

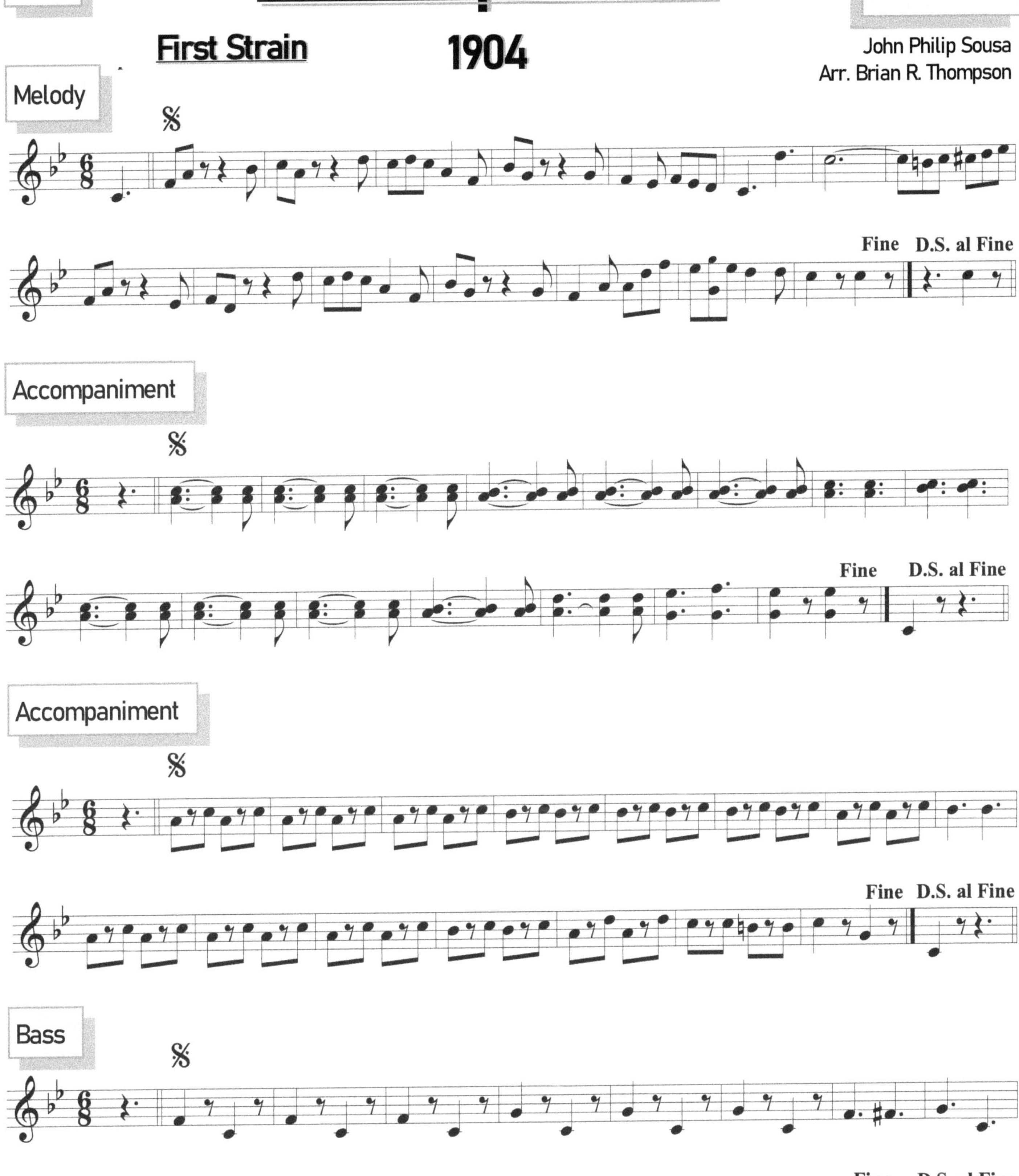

The Washington Post

Concert Oboe

Trio 1889

John Philip Sousa
Arr. Brian R. Thompson

33

The High School Cadets

Concert Oboe

33b

The High School Cadets

Concert Oboe

First Strain 1890

John Philip Sousa
Arr. Brian R. Thompson

Bass

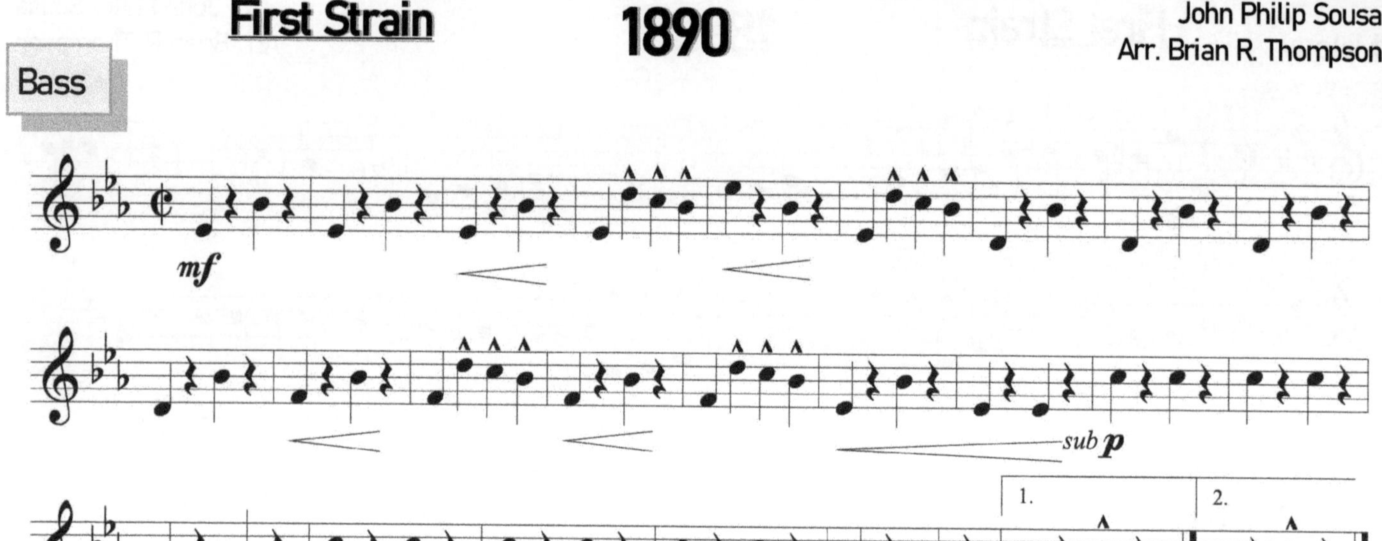

Homeward Bound (1891-2) — Intro

The Gladiator (1886) — Intro

www.ingramcontent.com/pod-product-compliance
Ingram Content Group UK Ltd.
Pitfield, Milton Keynes, MK11 3LW, UK
UKHW051134260726
13967UKWH00010B/3046

9 780359 860425